Languages of the World

Bengali

Harriet Milles

Heinemann
LIBRARY

Chicago, Illinois

www.capstonepub.com
Visit our website to find out more information about Heinemann-Raintree books.

To order:

☎ Phone 888-454-2279

⌨ Visit www.capstonepub.com to browse our catalog and order online.

Edited by Dan Nunn and Diyan Leake
Designed by Marcus Bell
Original illustrations © Capstone Global Library Ltd 2012
Picture research by Elizabeth Alexander

Originated by Capstone Global Library Ltd
Printed and bound in China by South China Printing
  Company Ltd

15 14 13 12 11
10 9 8 7 6 5 4 3 2 1

Library of Congress Cataloging-in-Publication Data
Milles, Harriet.
  Bengali / Harriet Milles.—1st ed.
     p. cm.—(Languages of the world)
  Text in English and Bengali.
  Includes bibliographical references and index.
  ISBN 978-1-4329-5835-0—ISBN 978-1-4329-5843-5 (pbk.)
1. Bengali language—Textbooks for foreign speakers—English.
2. Bengali language—Grammar. 3. Bengali language—Spoken
Bengali. I. Title.
  PK1662M55 2012
  491.4'482421—dc23   2011017915

Acknowledgments
The author and publisher are grateful to the following for permission to reproduce copyright material: Alamy pp. 7 (© David Grossman), 12 (© PhotosIndia.com LLC), 13 (© Louise Batalla Duran), 14 (© Danita Delimont), 17 (© Borderlands), 20 (© Borderlands), 22 (© Green Bangla), 23 (© Rphotos), 29 (© Samantha Nundy); Corbis pp. 16 (© Paul Hackett/In Pictures); Getty Images pp. 9 (Jewel Samad/AFP); 24 (Stu Forster); Getty Images for DAGOC p. 25 (Michael Steele); Photolibrary pp. 5 (Pawel Libera), 18 (Shehzad Noorani), 19 (Julio Etchart), 26 (Eye Ubiquitous); Photoshot p. 28 (Majority World/Mustafiz Mamun); Shutterstock pp. 6 (© Herr Petroff), 8 (© discpicture), 10 (© jaimaa), 15 (© Darrin Henry), 21 (© fritz16), 27 (© Joe Gough).

Cover photograph reproduced with permission of Getty Images (Asia Images Group).

Every effort has been made to contact copyright holders of material reproduced in this book. Any omissions will be rectified in subsequent printings if notice is given to the publisher.

Disclaimer
All the Internet addresses (URLs) given in this book were valid at the time of going to press. However, due to the dynamic nature of the Internet, some addresses may have changed, or sites may have changed or ceased to exist since publication. While the author and publisher regret any inconvenience this may cause readers, no responsibility for any such changes can be accepted by either the author or the publisher.

Contents

Bengali words in this book are in italics, *like this*.
You can find out how to say them by looking in the
pronunciation guide.

Bengali Around the World

Bengali is the main language of the region of Asia known as Bengal. The eastern part of Bengal is now the country of Bangladesh. The western part of Bengal is in India.

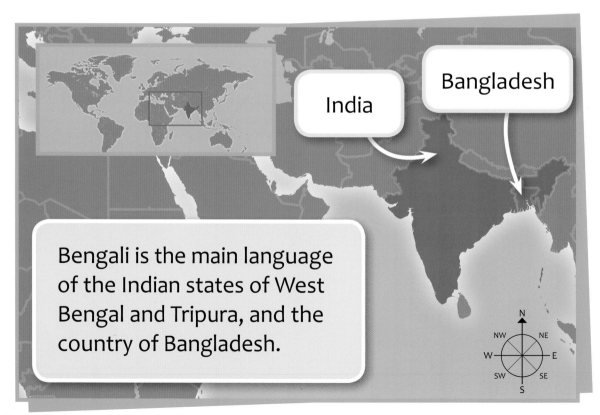

India

Bangladesh

Bengali is the main language of the Indian states of West Bengal and Tripura, and the country of Bangladesh.

Bengali food is famous throughout the world because it is spicy and delicious.

Bengali is the official language of Bangladesh. There are over 150 million people living in Bangladesh. After Hindi, it is the second most commonly spoken language in India.

Who Speaks Bengali?

Over 210 million people around the world speak Bengali as their main language. It is the world's fifth most widely spoken language, after Mandarin Chinese, English, Spanish, and Hindi.

People in this busy market sell flowers for weddings and special feast days.

Family life is very important for Bengalis.

The Bengali language is also called Bangla. Outside Bangladesh and India, there are Bengali speakers living in parts of Nepal, Singapore, Africa, Arabia, the United States, and the United Kingdom.

Bengali and English

Bengali uses a different alphabet than English. English is written on a line with the letters above it. Bengali is written along a line with the letters below it.

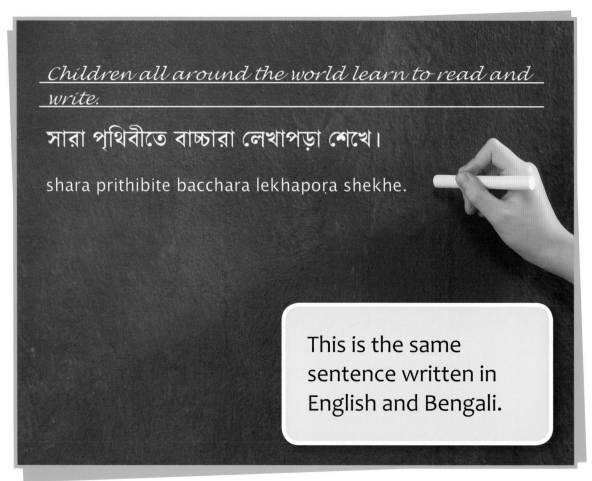

Children all around the world learn to read and write.

সারা পৃথিবীতে বাচ্চারা লেখাপড়া শেখে।

shara prithibite bacchara lekhapora shekhe.

This is the same sentence written in English and Bengali.

This is a busy doctor's office in Bangladesh.

Many Bengali people speak some English. There are words in Bengali that come from English words. For example, "doctor" is *ḍaktar*, "school" is *skul*, and "hospital" is *hashpatal*.

Learning Bengali

The English alphabet has 26 letters. Bengali script has many more letter symbols. So, how can you tell what Bengali script and symbols should sound like?

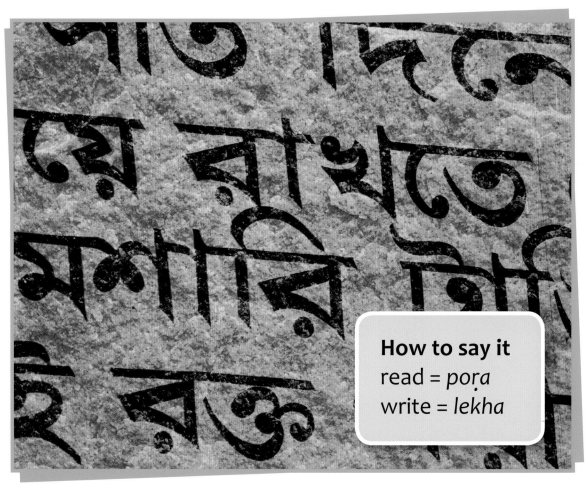

How to say it
read = *poṛa*
write = *lekha*

শুভ জন্মদিন ← Bengali script

śubhô jɔnmodin ← romanization

shubho jonmodin ← pronunciation

Happy Birthday ← English

How to say it
English = *Ingreji*

The best way for English-speaking people to learn Bengali is to see how the script would sound if it were written in the English alphabet. This is called "romanization."

11

Saying Hello and Goodbye

Bengali people may greet each other by saying, "*Nomoshkar.*" They may say, "*Tumi kæmon acho?*" This means "How are you?"

How to say it
hello = *nomoshkar*

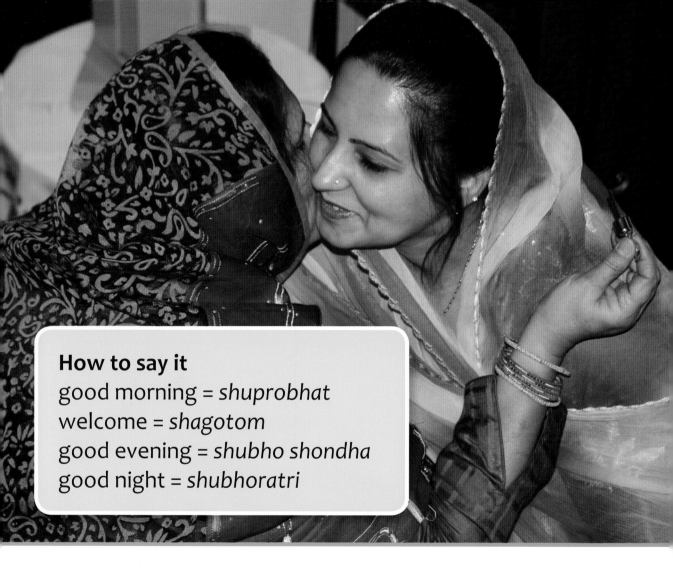

How to say it

good morning = *shuprobhat*
welcome = *shagotom*
good evening = *shubho shondha*
good night = *shubhoratri*

If you are visiting a Bangladeshi or Bengali family, they may say, "*Shagotom!*" which means "Welcome!" When it is time to leave, you might say, "*Abar dækha hobe,*" meaning "Goodbye, see you again."

Talking About Yourself

When you meet people for the first time, they may ask what your name is. Then you can say, *"Amar nam ..."* ("My name is ... ").

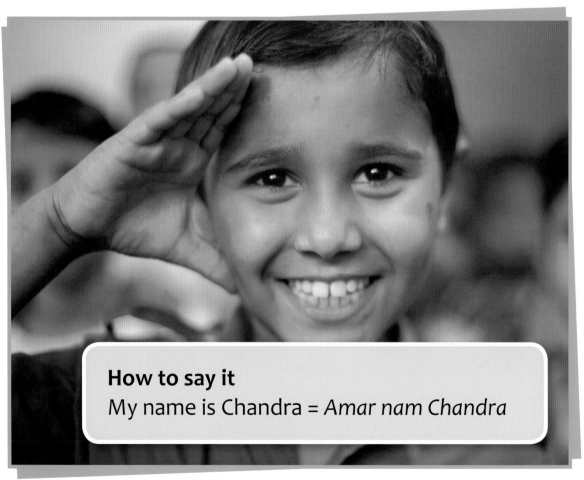

How to say it
My name is Chandra = *Amar nam Chandra*

Then they might ask you where you are from. You might say, "*Ami niu iyork thaki*" ("I'm from New York"). *Doya kore* means "please" in Bengali.

Asking About Others

It is polite to ask people about themselves. The first thing people usually ask is someone's name. You can say, *"Tomar nam ki?"* ("What is your name?")

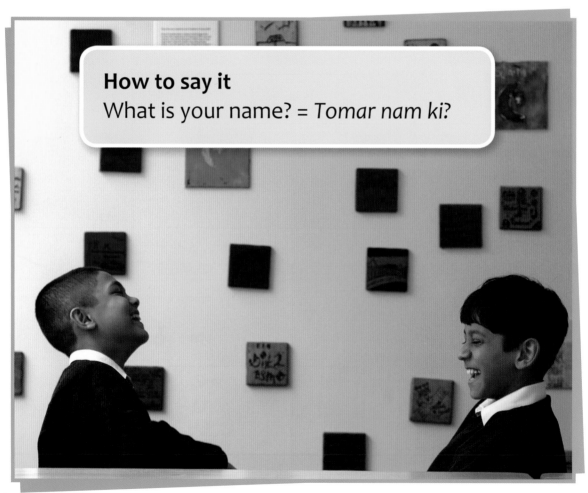

How to say it
What is your name? = *Tomar nam ki?*

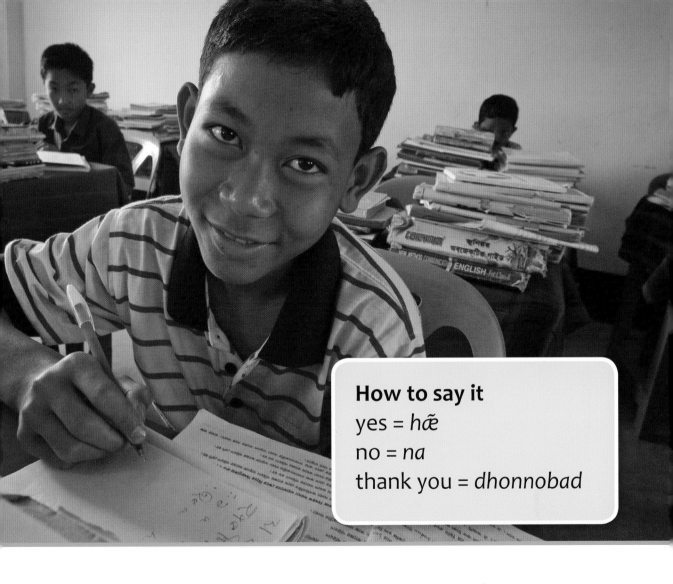

Then you might say, *"Tomar shathe poricito hoye ami khushi hoyechi"* ("I am pleased to meet you"). "Yes" in Bengali is *hæ̃*. "No" is *na*. The Bengali word for "thank you" is *dhonnobad*.

At Home

In country villages in Bangladesh, the houses are built of mud, straw, bamboo, or timber. The most important part of the home is the kitchen area. This is called the *ranna ghor*.

How to say it
village = *gram*
kitchen = *ranna ghor*

How to say it
house = *ghor*
rain = *brishṭi*

The Bengal region is one of the hottest places in the world. It also has a lot of rain. Some houses near rivers are built on stilts to prevent them from flooding.

Family

Bengali parents, children, aunts, uncles, cousins, and grandparents may all live close together. Their houses may be next to each other and they may share the family kitchen.

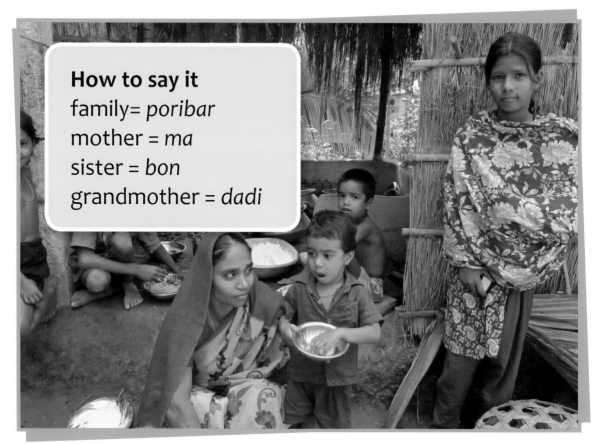

How to say it
family = *poribar*
mother = *ma*
sister = *bon*
grandmother = *dadi*

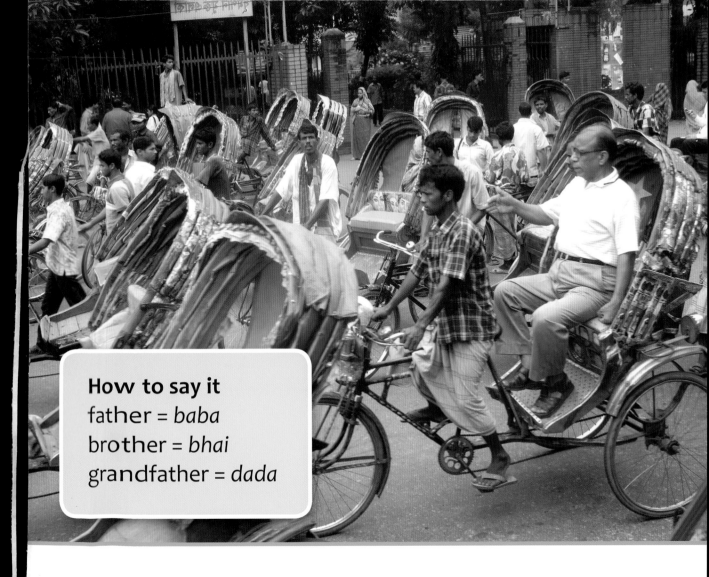

How to say it
father = *baba*
brother = *bhai*
grandfather = *dada*

Mothers and grandmothers may stay at home to do the cooking, cleaning, and washing. Fathers might do farming or work in towns or cities. A good way to travel to work is in a bicycle taxi called a rickshaw.

At School

In some village schools, children of all ages are taught in one big classroom. They learn to read, write, and do math. Sometimes they have classes outdoors, in the shade of trees.

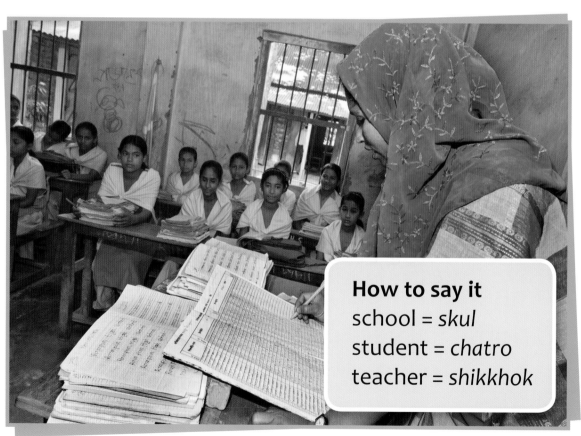

How to say it
school = *skul*
student = *chatro*
teacher = *shikkhok*

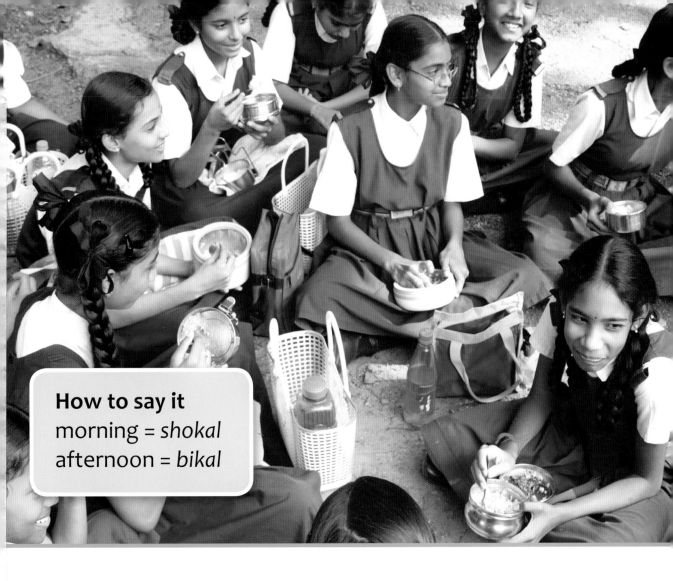

How to say it
morning = *shokal*
afternoon = *bikal*

After morning classes, the children may eat their lunch at school. They may also go home to eat. Some children from poor families may not go to school because they have to work.

Sports

The most popular games for boys in the Bengal region are cricket, which is similar to baseball, and soccer. Girls may play badminton or netball, but some enjoy playing cricket and soccer, too.

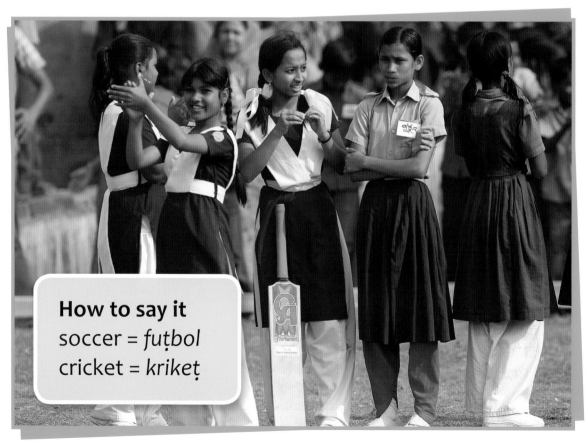

How to say it
soccer = *fuṭbol*
cricket = *krikeṭ*

Kabaddi is the national sport of Bangladesh. Two teams have to try to catch one another—and avoid being caught themselves—while holding their breath!

Food

Breakfast in Bengal or Bangladesh may be rice, chapatti (a flat piece of bread) with eggs, or some fish. People use their fingers to eat all meals.

How to say it
breakfast = *nasta*
rice = *bhat*
egg = *ḍim*

How to say it
vegetables = *shobji*
fish = *mach*
lunch = *dupurer khabar*

Bengali food is very spicy. Vegetable, chicken, or fish curry with rice is a popular lunchtime meal. People also love to drink *cha* (tea) all day long!

Clothes

Children in the Bengal region may wear T-shirts, shorts, or dresses. Girls may wear *shalwar kamiz* (a tunic and pants). After they are married, they wear a long piece of cloth called a *sari*.

How to say it
dress = *jama*
shoes = *juta*

How to say it
pants = *pænṭ*
shirt = *sharṭ*

In towns and cities, men may wear
pants and shirts. On special occasions,
Bengali men may wear a *kurta* (top)
and *dhoti*. The *dhoti* is a long piece of
white cloth wrapped around the waist.

Pronunciation Guide

English	Pronunciation of Bengali word
afternoon	*bikal*
Bengali	*bangla*
breakfast	*nasta*
brother	*bhai*
cricket	*kriket*
doctor	*daktar*
dress	*jama*
egg	*dim*
English	*Ingreji*
family	*poribar*
father	*baba*
fish	*maach*
good evening	*shubho shondha*
good morning	*shuprobhat*
good night	*shubhoratri*
goodbye, see you again	*abar dækha hobe*
grandfather	*dada*
grandmother	*dadi*
hello	*nomoshkar*
hospital	*hashpatal*
house	*ghor*
household	*khana*
How are you?	*Tumi kæmon acho?*
I am pleased to meet you.	*Tomar shathe poricito hoye ami khushi hoyechi.*
I'm from New York.	*Ami New York thaki.*
kitchen	*ranna ghor*

lunch	*dupurer khabar*
morning	*shokal*
mother	*ma*
My name is …	*Amar naam …*
no	*na*
pants	*pænṭ*
play	*khæla*
please	*doya kore*
rain	*brishṭi*
read	*poṛa*
rice	*bhat*
school	*skul*
shirt	*shart*
shoes	*juta*
sister	*bon*
soccer	*fuṭbol*
sports	*khæladhula*
student	*chatro*
tea	*cha*
teacher	*shikkhok*
team	*dol*
thank you	*dhonnobad*
vegetables	*shobji*
village	*gram*
welcome	*shagotom*
What is your name?	*Tomar nam ki?*
Where are you from?	*Tomar desh kothay?*
write	*lekha*
yes	*hæ̃*

1 = æk, 2 = dui, 3 = tin, 4 = car, 5 = pãc, 6 = choy, 7 = shat, 8 = at, 9 = noy, 10 = dosh

Find Out More

Books

Atkinson, Tim. *Discover India* (Discover Countries). New York: PowerKids, 2012.

Roy, Anita. *India* (Destination Detectives). Chicago: Raintree, 2006.

Thomson, Ruth. *Living in Bangladesh* (Living In...). North Mankato, Minn.: Sea to Sea, 2007.

Verma, Babita. *Star Children's Picture Dictionary: English–Bengali.* New Delhi: Star, 2006.

Website

www.timeforkids.com/TFK/kids/news/story/0,28277,1932891,00.html

See how floating schools are changing kids' lives in Bangladesh.

Index